I0818486

Next! (*new poems*)

Michael Gottlieb

Also by Michael Gottlieb

Collected Memoirs

Collected Poems

Selected Poems

Mostly Clearing

What We Do: Essays for Poets

I Had Every Intention

Dear All

Letters to a Middle-Aged Poet

The Dust (10th Anniversary Edition)

Memoir And Essay

The Likes of Us

Lost And Found

Careering Obloquy

Gorgeous Plunge

More Than All (with Ted Greenwald)

The Night Book

The River Road

Valu Pac

New York

The Blue Slope

Pantographic

96 Tears

Local Color/Eidetic Deniers

Next! (new poems)

Michael Gottlieb

chax
2026

ISBN: 978-1-946104-68-7

Library of Congress Control Number: application submitted.

Chax Press
6181 E 4th St
Tucson Arizona 85711

Chax Press books are supported in part by individual donors and by sales of books. Please visit *https://chax.org/membership-support/* if you would like to contribute to our mission to make an impact on the literature and culture of our time. Special thanks to Mary Ellen Bartholomew and André Spears for their generous and continuing support.

We thank our Art Director, Cynthia Miller, who contributes advice and support to all books Chax publishes.

for Charles Alexander

Contents

1. The

THE SHOW AND TELL TRIAL

the eternal *the*

the uncharacteristically sunny

the marches we stole

the once unthinkable
now commonplace

the low hanging
fruits of the crime

le mot unjust

the very last of the revenants
taking her ease in
the forecourt

the ungainly thresher
and the forlorn finery
and the farewell toast

the warp effect

the imposture syndrome

the modesty panel

the double-tap effect

THE UNDISPUTED REIGN

the sealed train

the devil's writing workshop
where they all met

the incorrigible shiplap
and all its pals
down below

the impresario
commandeering the lectern
to limn yet again
his debased
taxonomy of motives

the magneto
which refuses to charge
despite all
our entreaties

the old yes-comma-but
inevitably
coming round
for one more

the sequelae of deviation
from which arose
all our subsequent woe

the uncaring professions
and their uncanny grip
upon our joint
and several fates

the pretty pass
where we find
ourselves

the secret siding

THE SECOND-BEST PRACTICES

the hulking lorries
coming into view

the wave-action

the precursor materials
still discernable
beneath the unholy intarsia

the assets
illiquid yet
eerily buoyant

the undercarriage
of the argument

the central holding
flecked with recrimination

the threadbare plush
we were so happy to scorn

the hortatory

the fugitive footfalls

the so-called wealth effect
not that we would recognize it

the plain meaning

the evidence
mounting
the scaffold

THE LONELY AUTHORIZATION CONCEPT

the negligible impact
of his life-work
finally revealed

the doofus
among us

the historical maladies

the sublunary blather

the alarm
we all naturally felt
upon seeing you
in this state
of *even moment*
flushing us
with a secret surge
of salubrity
as we realized
no matter how low we sink
we still
look better than you

the so-called quiet periods
when we're really not supposed to trade

the catch-alls
and the dust-ups
and the hurried rites

the misfit ideation
you fancy unique to you

the particularized brooding
known to cognitive scientists
as morbid rumination

the accursed double-entry

the famous last words

the unblinking
and the cynosure

the straw that breaks
the camel's hair coat

the imitation
that breeds inanition

the difference
between pest
and pestilential

the ill
and the merely
ill-advised

the seldom unseen

the downright

the suddenly chastened Bluto

THE EVERLASTING PLAINT

the skeleton key

the difference
between soil
and dirt

the knock-out drops

the imposture
that spoke volumes

the self-tapping denial

the odds being
simply
even

the whisper-track
suggesting nothing less
than unconditional
surrender

the long-feared undertaking
we finally come to understand
is meant to be
our sole bequest

THE ROOKIE AND HIS ERRORS

the happy go lucky fer-de-lance

the apparently perfunctory

the disappointed hour

the fever swamps
where you find your true purpose

the looming imbroglio

the stuttering gunner

the visible hand
writing across
the dry-erase sky

the so-called perpetual care
we grudgingly allocate

the altogether stuporous

the last word
and the illusion of centrality
as seen from the suburbs
of the contretemps

the argument
from complexity
simply falling to pieces

the futile effort
to reconcile belief
in an omnipresent God

with the unavoidable reality
of endlessly unmerited suffering
in other words
theodicy

the dread side-slip

the prior bad acts

THE NONPAREIL VIEWS

the bit in our teeth

the long-awaited reckoning

the jerry-rigged windbreak

the 80/20 rule
that was
in truth
no more than
a Pareto distribution
of what I really
didn't want to
think about
anymore

the underlying pattern
like a woodgrain
eventually emerging
after decades
of wear and tear

the uncritical path
which led to
the great unraveling
which of course
was all
my fault

the toweringly wrathful

the rest of the band
coming in
on the downbeat

the occasional
adverse effect

the resigned bower

the last house
before the ragged defile

the awkward admission

the struggle sessions

the drummers
beating the tattoo

the welter

the tell
from hell

the onrushing present tense

the acid embrace

the booster seat
superseded
by the bucket seat
followed
as night follows day
by the ejection seat

THE INCURIOUS PRETENDER

the counting house
where we whiled away
our best days

the familiar miseries
as unavoidable
as unacknowledged

the underground streams
beneath the city
all still there

the least dear among us

the very fact
that we're having
this conversation

the pounding in the ears

the sorry lack of any incentive structure

the charging documents

the infrequently asked questions

the eternal *if only*
inevitably returning
settling upon our shoulders
like the dusk
whose shadows
lengthen apace

the last autumnal spate
of vainglory
we enjoyed

THE LAST OF THE HELLEBORES

the awful majesty of the law

the blithe misapprehension
that became
our most reliable
solace

the years spoke
of the accumulated toll

the inevitably unforeseen
so frankly uncanny

the animating principle

the quick lime and
the renowned slow burn
and the demurral and
the grid cracks
and the flyover
and the lip service economy

the mouth-feel of their words

the discards
we eagerly gathered up

the maladroit
and the unchurched

the abandoned winding tower
cloaked with secondary growth

the great retarding agent

the host triumphal

the grinning visage on
the obverse of the medal

the road builders
and their plans
for our future

the tumbling mats

the phrase
forever on our lips

the craquelure
in the finish

the great unwell
a host
whose number
we were soon
to join

the many-armed

the entire quarter rising up
that fateful night

2. There, That

THERE'S A LAST TIME FOR EVERYTHING

this is not the time
to put up your dukes

this weighs
upon us all

this admittedly
may seem a bit rich
coming from me

this actually
is an overture

this is not
what we
bargained for

this
my most
shameful bloomer

this is something
you can ignore
no longer

this little man
in my head
who won't shut up

this descent
into mandatory optimism

this was never
going to suffice

this I never
wanted to
burden you with

this is not what
success looks like

this refusal
to abide any longer

this
doesn't always
end badly
just usually

this will be
our little secret

THERE WAS A CHOICE

that's not quite
what I meant

there is no
such thing as
a good time
to ask that question

there's something
to be said
for that
just not
by me

that's exactly what
to our everlasting shame
everyone called it
back then

that
in fact
used to be
our motto

that abandoned
time signature

THAT DEBASED COINAGE

that was not a close call

those stubbed-out lines

that's called
giving me the back
of your hand

those were the tasks
we were set to
back when
we were assured
it made a difference
if we showed up

then still a young man

those years
we deemed
prima facie futile

then unaccountable
then some sort of expiry
then mayhap

there
by the rushes
and the sedge

that vital spark
that view of the vale
that sudden theft
of breath

THOSE ARE FIGHTING WORDS

there's a run rate
and then there's
a run-away rate

this was never my plan

this is not what
what some would call
a sunk cost

this is not
a second-order concern

this is not like
horseshoes and hand grenades

that's so funny
I forgot to laugh

THAT'S WHERE YOU LOST ME

this is why
it's called
command seating

that is
perfectly normal
at this stage

then fain to grasp

that's
the sad thing

then hesitating
upon the threshold

that was the evening
the words
'tell me more'
never passed my lips

THAT WHICH

that which
everyone including us
never failed to describe
as vanishingly unlikely
naturally enough
on the way back
to what we were told
was the rendezvous
we encountered
not once
not twice
not three times

this proved to be
just another
'priority dispute'

that folly
to assume
we wouldn't
end up
seeking to
redeem ourselves
for those deeds

those stolen
precious hours

that's the kind of thing
you never want to see

that is why
it really smarts

THOSE AND THEM

those who are lost
and those
who are disinclined
to forgive

those honeyed practiced lines
which once fell
upon receptive ears

that is not to say
that I did not
crave the spotlight
any less than you

that boughten glory

that's when
I started saying
that's not my job
even though
I didn't have a job

that craven miscalculation
that led me to warble
give me land lots of land
don't fence me in

this was not
my idea

this was
pure animus

that disco inferno

that royal road
not taken

that cascade of imposture

that's when
they started calling me
an imp of Satan

THIS I DIDN'T SEE COMING

this
is everything
I hate
in a quatrain

that's when
we learned
that liquor
is not quicker

those underlying facts
and those orphaned assets

that roughly hacked footpath
where one careless step
would be our last

there was a natural order
back then
those upstanding muggers
those carefree car stereo boosters
those dependably daffy
dope fiends
those poets

those mythy days
when the poets
masterless ronin
bestrode Chrystie St

those suddenly vivid
terms and conditions

that turned out

to be just the thing
we could never grasp

that is what
I finally realized
I'd been trying to say
all along

these poets who now dare
repeat themselves
how brave are they

there was no
farewell toast

this is the prosody
I thought
I'd leave for you

3. -Ing

ADMIRING THE VIEW

gamboling lightly
in the half-light

becoming ever more
like herself

settling upon her heirs

waiving none
of her right
title or interest

vexingly
true to life

unflinching
in that quest
to forget

nothing
becomes you
like nothing
at all

LAYING DOWN A MAGIC MARKER

fighting our corner

squaring up
for the next round

making a good fist of it

smoking us out

making a hash
of it

everything we told ourselves
we didn't need anymore

notwithstanding
anything else I might
have let pass my lips
in that moment
of weakness

importuning passage
at the gangway

carrying water for them

standing to

looking on

seeing off

looming over the crowd

taking a bead

sending down

dropping a plumb

hailing

topping off

trying me
too high

so carrying

an animating ideal
like words to live by
while all the while
pretending that
this is living

DYING IN THE LIVING ROOM

taking the conn

pouring it on

clobbering

fetching
giddily

braving the rapids

fueling their impotent ire

nattering on

skirting the worst
of the damage

dashing back and forth
before the front lines

presenting a vivid picture
to the parched imagination

coming eventually
to give new meaning
to the term
a race to the bottom

getting soused
at the progress bar

retailing that
carefully culled calumny

load-bearing arguments
in favor of forestalling

picking up
none of the slack

turning their hand
to anything
that really
doesn't need
doing

EVERYTHING HAS TO GO

impressing upon her memory
the imago
of her inamorato
like a coin
in the palm

confounding us
one and all

heaping portions
of just what
we knew
we didn't deserve

bearing in our arms
a sheaf
of anticipatory abnegations

knowing this much
and no more
never proved an impediment
when it came to
avoiding seeing
what was
right before our eyes

entertaining the notion

from eye popping
to eyewatering
in three weeks

dodging and burning
going all in

CALLING ALL CARS

hoving to

in the offing

lying in third place

sans any visible
supporting players

taking a shine to

taking no small
amount of pleasure

debouching at last
into the
brackish backwater
that is
our little world

doing the hard work
of hardly working

stunning advances
in the face
of daunting indifference

impugning
as the specialty of the house

ALL KIDDING ASIDE

shedding compunction
as we go

freely admitting
as if
we had
not a care
in the world

marking it
to market

our unassuming gait
that fooled
so many
for so long

as if god fearing

taking a lazy bite
of the low hanging fruit
from the decision tree

WHERE IS YOUR STING

something
finally akin
to a keen interest

being “read in”
in this use-case
means we do indeed
need to say
we’re sorry
after the after-action
is duly not acted upon

regaling them
with tales
of the transmigration
of our youthful souls

it had all the makings
of a descent into a
war of all
against all
which was
of course
our fondest hope

NOT FOR NOTHING

giving the people
what they don't want
that's always been
our highest calling

4. When, Where, What

WHO TALKS LIKE THAT ANYMORE

who doesn't
love a parade

who was a trial
frankly

whoever would have thought
that someone like you
could end up
somewhere like this

who was
the one person
who knew
what jamais vu
really meant to you

who has never quite
grasped the concept
of relevant boundary conditions

who
among us
doesn't look
altogether fallible
at this age

who used to frequent
these haunts
now haunts
our thoughts

who speaks for this poet

WHAT IS TO BE UNDONE

whereon

where once
almost nothing stirred

which has met
with something
other than
universal approbation

what did we
really know
about what
we were about
back then

what's left
to be said

what the wreckage
never fails to serve up

what
makes you think
you know better

what we once deemed
beneath us

what we convinced ourselves
was altogether
too much to bear

what is not dispositive

and never could be

who she called
her insignificant other

who is unfit for purpose

who did them down
and why

who is ill-disposed
to see you

who has
the last word
which is
squalor

what
your impoverished imagination
could never conjure

what you weren't
watching all that closely
while you were
whiling away
all that time

what we lack
bringing us back
again and again
to this
fly-blown pavilion
thronged with
disappointed suitors

what comes back
to bite me

WHAT DON'T WE HAVE TO LOSE

what we used to call
character recognition

what we've
resolutely declined
to address

what she means
when she says
I'm not proud
of what we did

what he deserved
and why
he never got it

what we've always said
we'd prefer to spend
our days doing
now that
there's nothing else
to do

what we
were always
spoiling for

why the opposite
of rest
is not unrest

WHEN AND WHAT

when quantity
had a quality
of its own

what
now

what
I can stand
today
as opposed to
what
I stood for
yesterday

what is priced-in
inevitably
when we say
there was once a time
when we were so sure
we could assay
the joint and several
futures of
our fated
friends

WHAT'S NOT ON OFFER

what possibly
could possess you
to believe
you could pull off
a stunt like this

what are not
words to live by

what we keep out of the sun

what then
was written about
so rarely

what grew to
its current
monstrous proportions
while we were busy elsewhere

when you finally
spoke up

when the little voice
in your head
starts to cough
alarmingly

what else
could any
of this
be about

why don't you

ask him
yourself

why did we
not end up
just like him

what we thought
we had
left remaining

what a legacy
you have bequeathed us

what those days
we would damn
as a mere
nota bene

WHAT THEN PLUMMETS

what was muddied

what came to be ensconced

what loiters in the updraft

what you're really saying
when you say
thank you
for your honesty

what must needs be endured

what we really desire now

what we mean
when we say
with great powerlessness
comes great irresponsibility

5. To

A CONVINCED FLAT EARTHER

to skate
too close

to row back

to claw back
the ill-gotten gains

to claim
this land

to demob

to delist

to despoil

to entertain
incomprehension

to start to say
something that you know
you will regret
to the end
of your days
only to realize
that you don't
need to actually say it out loud
because
everyone already
knows just how you feel

to self-soothe
with sandpaper

THE FIRST PAST THE GATE

to all appearances

to delaminate

to disport

to decorticate

to display
the humble mien

to comport

to maintain the decorum
appropriate to the occasion

to be far eclipsed

to at least entertain
the notion
that we have
no idea at all
which end is up

to accept our lot
even though
it's not a lot

to beat
the band
within an inch
of their miserable lives

to my way
of thinking
as if this
was anything
I'd ever be caught dead
thinking about

to roundly descry
immediately
and then unhesitatingly
take up with
gusto

to exhibit no ambition
whatsoever with regard
to that attribute
of our core content

to be obliged
to witness
that alien creed
ascending
to the heights

to be anointed
our byword and hissing

VEER YAW AND PITCH

to besmirch

to say
this far
and
no further

to be sure

to establish
a simulacrum
of suzerainty

to lie abed
to all hours

to round upon them

to worry
unto unravelling

to harry
mercilessly

to self-seed
as if
sown with doubt

to keep the dust down

to cover the mirrors

to liken ourselves to
– as if
we really
did like
ourselves

6. And

CUNNING AND CAREERING

and if
all was said
and done

and if
there was a moment
when I thought
by lending a hand
it would make a difference

and if they
are the only
ones left standing
then
we're really
in trouble

and why not
I always used to say

and would you care
as they used to say
to make this interesting?

THE FUGITIVE FOOTFALLS

and the lands beyond

and the savage breast

and the heaving sea

and the law
of the excluded middle

and all his pomps

and what
what we used to know as
service with a smile

and your coevals too
if you admit to any

and what price
pray tell
would you
not be willing
to pay?

and the parting-out

and
took
and
mistook

and who
may I say
is calling?

AND SO IT BEGINS

and only just

and we're off

and still
they come on
without an apparent
care in the world

and in the end
it mattered not

and so it came to pass
that we lost
if not quite everything
then just enough
for it to
become altogether clear
not just what we owed
and to whom
but how unlikely
it was that
we'd ever be able
to pay back
even a portion
of this principal

and this
is what
we've been
reduced to

7. No

NOTING FOR FUTURE REFERENCE

no one
asked for this

not
next to nothing
but nearby
instead

no interest
so no conflict
that's how
we do compliance
around here

not fire-proof

not unlike

not to be
undone

not just discomfited

no joy
in the morning

not on my
side of the street

not
altogether delightedly

no
but still

not so

NOT REALLY A SURETY

no matter
what everyone else
is saying about you

not everything
always goes
up and to the right

no end
to this foolishness

not all that fetid
considering

no right to repair
this wrong

nothing
to see here

not nearly

there's no
end of days
scheduled
for today

8. Don’t

DON'T TRY THIS ANYWHERE EXCEPT AT HOME

don't step
don't repeat

don't you
just want
to scream

don't say
funny story
ever

don't try that
on me
again

don't always
seem so
eager

don't stop
doing that
just because
I asked you to

don't they
just make you
want to throw up
your hands

don't the odds
look like
they are lengthening

don't you think

we've paid enough
by now

don't you agree

don't I wish

9. Such

SUCH DISOBLIGING

such like

such a fool

such a one

such a pity

such repining

such pointless palaver

such a capacious portmanteau

such is
what we're
reduced to

10. Now

THE HERE AND NOW

now it can be told

now I am
truly lost

nowadays
we don't
know better

by now it's
probably
too late

now I wish
I could have
helped you more

now and then
I can't help
but reflect upon
how all this
is naturally
all my fault

now and forever more

now is not the time

now you tell me

11. Un-

UNCOUNTED MULTITUDES

unreasoning

unalloyed

unheard
that morning

unmarred
for the moment

the unabashedly
unambiguous

unsaid
in the interest of
underscoring

unsigned
as if
we should know
who'd pen
something like this

undone
by the events
in question

uncovering everything
the mechanism
was meant
to mask

undressed
for success

simply untold

the undead
who would gladly
leave us alone

unseasoned
at least
by any experience

unthinking
as usual

12. In

CUI SONNY BONO

in the matter of

in the instance

in the event

in arrears
as always

in the mind of the suborned

in no one's
best interest

in the meantime
we're left
with *this*

in all likelihood
this will end
just as badly
as the last time

in all honesty

in the off chance

in later years
he was often
to be seen
lingering along the corniche
by that stretch
of riverfront
long-since claimed

by a palisade of glass towers
where once
in desolate lots
ranks of tractor trailers
every night
stood ready and waiting

UNJUST ENRICHMENT

in the
shallows

in a manner
of speaking

in much
the same

in the end
we stood him
a decent lunch

in another time
or place
I would have
heartily agreed

in the way
of things
not often enough
left unsaid

in the end
wouldn't you say
we all pay
but some of us
have a higher
credit limit

“MORE RUBBLE LESS TROUBLE”

in the next enfiladed lee
soi-disant
figures
beckoning
with broad gestures

in the
not-so-great room

in that asset class

in this heavy weather

insensibly caparisoned

insuperable
and thus unsupportable

in the third
and last reading

in the surf
the churned-up chum

in her own hand
which
naturally
we all recognized

13. We

WE SET THE PAR VALUE

we got creamed
as simple as that

we thought
it was
a good idea
at the time

we thought
at first
you were
happy to see us

we thought
it was high time
to have this conversation
with you

we credited
all of your claims
but still
found you wanting

we really didn't expect
you'd still
be around

we assumed
you were that kind of guy

thusly
we adorned you
back then

then we caught you at it again

MONOPSONY NO MORE

ours by right
title and
lack of interest

ours
by dint
of the hours
we wasted on this

our jollies

up to
our neck

our spell
in this joint

our sundry
sorry sobriquets

as is
our wont
when it comes to
talking about
what we want

it is
our pleasure
to serve you
this dish
cold

AS WE SPEAK

we are foregathered here

but before we begin

we the unready
the unwilling
the unable

we had no way of knowing

the way
we used
to present

we came to realize
the reason that
we don't much
like one another
is because
we're really
so alike
each other

we call it
tearing off
the band aid

we will all
have to take
a haircut

can we join
a members club
if we don't have

all our members

we gradually
grew alive
to the settled truth
that had descended
upon us–

WE SOUGHT THE SHORE

we recognized them
by their distinctive plumage

we saw
the way they
picked and chose
among us

we remained convinced
even at this late date
that perseveration
was the path
to preservation

we found
ourselves wondering
if they
were considering
selling us
for parts

we thought
this is as bad
as it can get

then
we caught sight
of the towering clouds
making their ineluctable approach

14. They, She, He

A BAD THROW

his safe word
was Mosler

he was
in the final respect
a smaller than life
figure

he was not
simply too good
for this world
that was not
his problem

he didn't actually
live under a rock

he only pretended
to be
a convinced
apostate

he had signally failed
to flag
that fatal flaw
back in
the design-phase

he came to be
tarred with that moniker
forever after

his career
came to be seen

by the rest of us
as one endless
amended complaint

he wasn't always
such a good hater

he tried to
throw his life away
but he was
a bad throw

HER FINGER PAINTS WERE ALL OVER THIS

she blew
hot and hot

she clocked him
a good one

she was always pricing
us into the valuation

she showed us
her signature font

she was not
able to tolerate us
at that dosage

she's the kind of person who
we used to say
deserved everything
that was coming to her
so we really shouldn't
have been surprised
when she ended up
with everything

ANIMAL MINERAL VEGETABLE

he didn't need to learn
how to take a punch
there was so much
on-the-job training

he was once adept
at bristling
with indignation

he was pretending
not to follow along

he didn't used to
suffer geniuses gladly

certainly
he has all his faculties
it's just that of late
some seem
on sabbatical

THEIR ANIMAL SPIRITS

they certainly did not
cover themselves in glory
that afternoon

they were the ones
not made
of sterner stuff

they also eschew
who sit and wait

their
unassimilated
misapprehensions

their portfolio decisions
weighing them

they will always claim
they did it
for the good
of the sport

their joint and
several futures
thrown
off the back
of the sled

15. A

A NOT UNCRITICAL MASS

a rump session

a non-performing loan

a white marriage
of inconvenience

a cuffing
undeniably
undeserved
and yet

a HO scale
train of thought
leading us
resolutely
to the sorts of conclusions
which while
implausibly
over-provisioned
mayhap might not be
so ill-proportioned
that they too
don't betray
that all-too familiar
rank impoverishment
of impulse

A GRAB-AND-GO MINDSET

a ranging shot

a big-character poster

a stopper
for every bottle

a sudden
yet altogether
predictable decline

a carelessly cobbled-up
illusion of perspectival compression
within which
all manner
of ambit
for just the sort
of inadvertently erected
permission structure
we still are obliged
to navigate through
for some reason
ups and decides to
hove into view

a school of thought
that's been
deemed
by one and all
as irredeemably
misaligned
if not downright
malign

a head-snapping
leave-taking

a failure to thrive

a proper dust-up

a convincing impression

a shrewd blow

a sudden
show of hands

a bad mood board
a don't look book

SEEING IS BELIEVING

as if
you knew
better

as if
no one
had even
noticed you

as if
there was
a mote
in your eye

as if
you had a clue

as if
there was
any rejoicing
in this

as if
it was not
a non-trivial number

A SORT OF FEEDSTOCK

a sort of
feedstock
for our
underfed imaginations

a dab hand
at this sort
of sleight of hand

an unappreciated unguent

a bumper car crop

a grim smile
espied from
the driver's side mirror

a late model coupe
from back when
every fall
there was
a new model-year

a turn round the course
after which
we were ready
to mix it up again

a medal struck
to commemorate
that great day
when finally
we found ourselves
cleared

to take the tiller

a tension bar

an unholy alliance

a sore winner

a night to forget
untroubled by
that storm to the west
which dissipated
before reaching us
a kind of providential
suspended sentence

a restorative
quickly quaffed
during the interval

a yearslong scheme
that came to tears
as so often happens

a song on our lips

a thumping majority

a confused torrent

a roundhouse punch

a kind of registry
of abandoned asseverations

a real doozy

ALL ASUNDER

a lush worker

a place of ill fame

a regnant reality
inveigling us
into stiffening our resolve
whilst simultaneously
inviting us
to loosen
our stays

a motto like
effectiveness-and-efficiency
or land-and-expand

a burning reason

a grave mismatch

a so-called proffer session

BUYING THE DIPS

a walk-off homer
in the walk-in refrigerator

an overwhelming
over and under

an outcome
devoutly
to be wished for

a self-collar

a proper cock up

a considerable lack
of adhesion

a negligible contribution
to our weal

a rivalrous pair

a work brigade
which we came
to understand
the hard way
was nothing less than
a punishment battalion

as we move
from fluidity
to loquacity
just upstream
of the long-feared

inevitable
descent
into garrulity

an inessential tremor

an iron law
for us too

16. It

IT ISN'T WHAT IT ISN'T

it was on
the tip
of my tongue

it was here
a minute ago

it's a
charm bracelet
offensive

it's one thing to be
an agent of the Devil
it's another thing to be
the agent for the Devil

but it's not all
about me

IT RETURNS

it met
my expectations
at the
crossroads

it comes
upon us all
eventually

it comes
and goes
not unlike you

it was
a disuse case

it wasn't
a cul-de-sac
it was dead end

it was not
a nice to have
it was a nice
to get rid of

it was
a mutual aid pact
like any other

it was
a case of magical
what-were-you-thinking

it's called

selling you the dummy

it's called
getting you to 'yes'

it's called
a bully pulpit
for a reason

it's called
the last-and-final
for a reason

IT SLICES IT DICES

it was
a rare moment
of calm
the kind
that never
bodes well

it was not
lost upon us

it was a way
of saying
isn't this
what you've always
been asking for

it becomes you
in fact
it's taken over

it was
deemed
an end
unto itself
and so
like so much
those days
it promptly
ended

LET IT NOW BE UNSAID

it is far from certain
and getting decidedly
farther

it's never
a sure thing

it just rolled
off my tongue

it quite nearly
brought me to tears

it was nothing
you said
it never is

it shone forth
with a light
so pellucid
and lambent
in the way
it acknowledged
all our halting entreaties
and our quite nearly
sincere protestations
that it's still hard
to believe
it could
have originated with
the likes
of you

IT WAS

it was
falling in sheets

it was
raining blows

it was
a negative option play

it was
never
lost on us

it was
a don't
ask me anything
session

it was a
reversion
to the mean
spirited

it was
bound to get worse
before
it got worse

IT'S A DOOZY

it was entirely
within your gift
to provoke
that sort of
response

it always
pencils out
to more than you'd expect
if you think of it
less as a loss
or some iteration of shrinkage
but instead
the surviving tenancy
of those
damned-up moments
of indulgence
which always threatened
to topple over into
so-easily calumnied excuses
for summoning
our version of the authorities
in your case
a call-to-arms
for your patented amor-propre
which perhaps it's time to give
a not-very-well-deserved rest

17. You

YOUR AD HERE

you remind me
of me
and I wish
you would
do something
about that

you don't say
and you
won't stop

you never know
and that's always
been a problem

you can't really
call this
easy listening

you are
all too you
as usual

you have questions
I wish I had answers

you really
did me a dirty
there
even if it was
back in the 80s

you could make out
his art school training

at the opening
in the way
he appeared
not to recognize
you from Adam

you only thought
we were pretending
to listen
but we showed you

you can quote me
but then
after all these years
you'd have to
learn my name

you know
of course
this means war

YOUR PROBABLY WONDERING

you're probably wondering
why we asked you here

you really may not
be doing yourself
any favors here

your proud schemes and
your mighty works
may fool the others
but we see
behind you
past the
your gaggle of credulous lienholders
and that ginned-up troupe
of dumb-show lay analysands
there's a slick
of no-longer
suspended disbelief
its sheen of reproof
gleaming dully
under the kliegs
unspooling now
closely following you
like a faithful sidekick

YOUR PAL MOREY

your pal Morey
always so big
for souvenirs
we came to call him
memento Morey

YOU DO YOU

you truly are
a thin client

you are forever
lacking standing
just like us

you didn't duck
that's why
you ended up
like this

you're getting a traumata
and you're getting one
and you're getting one

you too beggar belief

you are indeed
the incompletist

you are forgetting
that we cast you
in the role of sidekick

you are not
having a moment
because
it's not yours

you can't imagine
what it feels like
that's my job

you heard it here last

your body
is not necessarily
your friend

thy rods and thy cones
they comfort me

NOT YOUR BEST WORK I FEAR

your remaining
hopes and fears
the ones you
wanted to believe
could inoffensively
potter about
like superannuated pensioners
in their allotments
now instead
we see everywhere
sleeping rough
beneath every blighted hoarding

you could call it
wire-management
for your inner life
but then
there'd have to be
some sort of
chase or cableway
to stow
all those untidy impulses
that every evening
snake across
the stained cement
of this abandoned storage unit
where we've
been obliged
to immure
what was once called
your imagination

your old friends
those

still out
in other words – ambulatory
who once
thanked you
for your honesty
now wonder
what next will
come out
of your mouth
as we recognize
that you too
now tarry
in those limpidly-lit dells
where your kind
can frolic
in a perfected
no-fault vainglory
inhibitionlessly
ensuring that finally
the rest of us
know exactly
what you think

18. I

A TONER-STAINED WRETCH

a toner-stained wretch
am I

I more than
any of you
am not worthy

I'm sure
I had it right here
a minute ago

I stole all these
fair and square

I needed you to know

I had that feeling

I worked
long and hard
to get all these things
I don't deserve

I AM THE TRIER OF FACT HERE

I claim this land for

I'll put it all on Red

yes I think
I will have another

but I did not realize
I'd be called on
for seven feats of strength

"you're telling me
I'm losing to this guy?"

I really wanted
to say goodbye

I shaved my head for *this?*

I am here
with your cancer answer

I'M HIGH ON LIFE

I'm high on life

I wanted to call
a time-out

I never failed
not to notice

I need it now
more than ever

I'm sure
I put it
right over there

honest officer
I don't know
how this got
in my pocket

of course
I didn't want
to tell you

I couldn't wait to be finished

and I could pretend no longer

I'm not ok with that
I never was

I thought
I was just
along for the ride

I didn't have the heart

if you can't see my mirrors
I can't see you

I LOVE THEM ALL

I love them all
cyan
magenta
yellow
and the holy key

so I asked them
to run a panel

I've heard that one
more than once

I'm not so glad
we had
this conversation

I once stood
where
you stand
now

I ROAMED

I roamed
the streets
and brought
you back
this

if I had a dollar
for every time
someone asked me that
I'd still
be poor

I agree
you had to
do something
different
but this
was not it

"I'm interested
in changing the world
and also
drugs I can smoke"

I used to say
I'm up for
almost
anything

I wanted to raise my hand

I had a hankering

I want to believe
that I did try

IF I KNEW THEN

I held no truck with that

I almost had a conniption

"I progress as I digress"

I can't top that

I wish
I had
better news

I wish I could say
I never believed
any of it

all the while
I was plotting
your discomfiture

I'd rather find myself
dead in a ditch

I'm not a fan
I never was

if it was up to me
I wouldn't let him
carry my ditty bag

I know
you are
but what
am I?

I WASN'T SURE IF

I wasn't sure if
I didn't understand it
or I just hated it

if I have to think
then I think not

I'd like to think so
or I used to

I stopped
trying to be witty
all the time

if I'm rubber

I wouldn't if
I couldn't

I lost my shit
at the convenience store

I wish I knew
how often I say
I wish I knew

I KNOW THERE'S A PONY

I know there's a pony
in there
somewhere

I have a hard stop
at the bottom of the hour

I have
no earthly idea

I'm taking my ball
and going home

I always wished
I'd said that

I can see it
clearly now
as if
it was yesterday

I wanted
to be able to say
that you've still
got it going
I really did

I'm tired
of reminding him
how much
he's forgot

I can
take him

or leave him

I used to know better
than to mutter
things like that

I kid
because
I love

I WON'T

I did not think
we should let
our successors-in-interest
decide this

I will
if I may
refer you
to my referred pain

I was glorying in their scorn

I was busy improving my mind

I was going to say
I won't
trouble you again

I'M GOING TO MEET MY MAKER SPACE

I can always say
I went down fighting

"I feel like I'm dying
but I'm afraid I won't"

I knew
I wasn't at 100%

I guess
I'm really not
helping my case here

I ask myself
the same question

Thanks, Joe!

(*an essay*)

1. PUTTING THE TERROR BACK IN TERRIBLE

As I worked on these poems and started to share them, reading them at readings, seeing the first of them published, I found myself asking myself some questions. The same questions I ask myself, maybe all of us ask, as new work goes out the door.

For one: are these any good? I certainly worked on them pretty hard, as hard and as long, and through as many drafts as I ever do, but what do I know? They could be terrible. I have no idea. These kinds of questions are my familiars, arising always around now.

But then, some new ones: will people get this? This Brainard-brainstorm of mine, will it remind people of him? Will it seem simple, maybe even lovely, but also, possibly, mysterious? Or, maybe my friends will say to themselves – or even to my face – Michael, you've finally lost it. In other words, not simple but simple-minded?

Or, it occurs to me now, might no one even notice? Will this seem just more of the same? More of me? When will he ever change? When will he stop repeating himself? And didn't he use that very phrase, that tiresome ten-dollar-word, and that one and that one, back in the Nineties?

I don't have a day job anymore. Now I can work all day. I tell myself that I'm so lucky. I have all this time to write. Look at how much work I did, in not much more than a year. When I was younger, this would have taken me years and years… putting in an hour at five in the morning, before heading off to the office; or sitting down for an hour or so late at night, at this same table, back when the children were small, after they went to bed.

And it also seems important, for some reason, to assert – or is it attest, or, perhaps, asseverate – that at this stage in life, I do still have a lot of energy. But don't a lot of people go through this right, after they retire?

…I'll do this and then I'll do that and, oh, I have so many projects. Look at me, I'm still hale and hearty. But how long can this last? Who's to say this isn't some sort of Indian summer? A blaze, its final flaring.

2. NEXT?

I was in a bar on Mott Street and I was young. I was talking to someone, and after a while it became obvious that we weren't clicking. Actually, she realized it first. For me it became clear when she called out, ringingly, broadcasting to one and all, the establishment at large: 'Next!'

I had been dismissed.

So it was that I found myself, not so very long ago, shortly before writing any of these new poems, muttering the same to myself as I sat at my desk. Not because I pined for those days, or that young woman, but because I was stuck. What was supposed to come next?

Of course, it wasn't as if I hadn't been busy. I had been very busy. No one could claim otherwise.

But now, clearly, I had too much time on my hands. There was no gainsaying that. So, after giving the matter some thought, in the summer of 2023, I took a good hard look around and decided it was high time to do something about the disaster that was my bookshelves. They were a mess. And then there were the piles. Books everywhere, on every flat surface, including the floor. Teetering piles, ominous, looming.

Great. Now I had something to do.

The thing is, as I worked on this project, I realized that in all likelihood in a few more years I would again run out of shelf space, and then what? I looked down at the bottom set of shelves. On that row sit boxes of manuscripts and collages and papers and correspondence which, for a reason that escapes me still, I've never gotten it together to throw out.

Maybe, finally, this was the time to toss them all, I thought. I could just take all sixty, seventy odd boxes to the transfer station. That might be the simplest solution. Done.

It also occurred to me at this point that, possibly, that all this activity, all of this careful project management, measuring and cutting shelves and alphabetizing all of those books I hadn't looked at in years, nay since I'd first acquired them twenty, thirty, forty, fifty years ago, which now I was engaged in, as I laid-in new shelving and sorted – for the first time, for the very first time in my life, tried to organize my books – and then restacked all of them, was in fact no more than yet another pathetic attempt to avoid answering a different question, a version of that ringing alarm that girl in the bar had sounded so many years ago.

Next? What was supposed to happen next?

I'd been avoiding that question for years, hadn't I? I'd been doing a lot of writing, but I hadn't written any new poetry. Essays, memoirs, introductions, adaptations, yes. But no poems – save for a long Covid poem. Nothing for four years or so. What was next?

3. HAVERING OVER THIS

It all started more than fifty years ago, when I came to New York. I would pick up scraps of paper lying in the street. Back then, the streets weren't all that tidy, especially in the parts of town where I found myself. I look at the collages I made back then, and the found material they're composed of; those streets, that's where they came from. All that paper, just lying on the sidewalk, in the gutter. I walk those same streets now, all these years later, a veritable old man, but there's nothing there. There are no more financial printers, no more customs expeditors or warehousemen or handbill men. That must be why. Those scraps, that's what I wrote upon first.

Then, after a few years, I started making sure I always left home with an index card in my pocket. I've held onto them too, God knows why. Then, a few more years further along, I started going about with a jotter. Those were cunning little leather goods. They held four or five cards, one tabbed in place conveniently, ready for use. Then I got a nicer one, from Bottega Veneta. That's how fancy I fancied myself. For years now, of course, like everyone else, I've been reduced to my phone's Notes function.

Notwithstanding all that, since the beginning, back when all I had was wastepaper, nothing, when it comes to the way the words turn into poems, has changed.

The words get written down. The words I see, I hear, that arrive. And when there are enough of them, I make of them a list. Of course a list. And eventually I turn them onto a page. Like releasing a flock into a pasture. Or maybe a herd. Possibly a pack. Then I print it out and give it the once-over.

After a while, I'll cross out one word, it's become clear that it doesn't belong, and move another from the page's bottom to the top. And one word will suggest another. A single word will turn into a phrase. Then I will take that marked-up page and retype it. Now, there's a second draft.

A phrase will need to be a sentence; a line become a stanza. They will indicate as much. And then there will be a third draft. And a fourth, and a fifth, and eventually several dozen. And then, when there seems to be no more to be done, there will be a poem.

But one thing I never worried about was what these poems were to be about. I still don't. They will become what they want to be. Whatever is lurking inside of me, that I don't want to talk about, am trying hard not to think about, will emerge. Will come out to play, will declare itself eventually, and of course it will have its demands. They always do.

But all those drafts? And all these boxes? I never threw them out. Why?

I remember Jackson Mac Low telling me, when he sold his papers, how bereft he felt when they came and took everything away; positively distraught. Would I react similarly? I tell myself that I'd like to find out.

4. AND SO

That feeling that comes over me when I sit down to write, when did that start? That sense that, despite how hard I try to make it for myself by changing the rules, or telling myself that I am changing the rules, it doesn't matter: I think I know what I'm doing. If I'm not all that special, not terrifically good at this, at least I'm competent. Aren't I? How it came to steal over me. But no, maybe not competency. Complacency, perhaps. And, possibly, pernicious.

As I cast about at the end of 2023, trying to figure out what to do next, what to do *differently* compared to whatever it was I had done last, because it had become too easy – hadn't it? – I came to a halt. I was quite stuck, altogether stymied. And, to make things rather worse, having recently worked several compilations of previously published work, each brought to press by the lovely and thoughtful Charles Alexander, every single way that I had tried, in the past, to solve for this – just this problem – was fresh in my mind. So now what? What to do next? And by now, of course, I had several years-worth of these piles of words. List upon list. Lists I had been ignoring studiously. So much precursor material, waiting, lying there, obdurate, adamantine.

But not a lot of ideas. In fact, no ideas whatsoever. Long lines? Done that. Short lines? Done it. No punctuation? Done it. No caps? Done that too. Let the grim in? Enough already with that. Try for optimistic? No, not again.

How can I keep from repeating myself – from making it easy on myself – because unless I constructively make it different, it will be easy, and if it's easy, then 'competency' wins, and all this becomes an exercise in having fun. And that's not what this is supposed to be about. It can't be.

As I grew more desperate, I found myself thinking more and more of my first book. Those poems were all chance-generated; the product of other operational processes too, rules that I created for myself. Maybe that's what I needed to go back to. As I looked over the pages where they had recently been excerpted, in the beginning of the first of that series of books that Charles had just published, something else came back to me: how freeing it felt to write those poems. A feeling I'm not sure I ever felt again.

5. ADMIT IT

But maybe the smart thing to do is simply stop. Admit it: there is no good reason to keep on and there hasn't been for years. This is why you can't figure out what comes next. Concede. You are no better than your friends who stopped years ago, or should have. You might be a few years younger, and always considered yourself somewhat cooler – which meant what? That you were going out to the Pep or Danceteria or Hurrah or the Mudd Club while they were sitting in their apartments, listening to opera – but so what?

But stopping is not the same as quitting.

Maybe, you could just pause for a while. Try that out for size. Catch your breath. Hopefully no one will ask you why. Like: what's the matter, are you out of breath? Have you been so terribly busy?

On the other hand, quitting does have attached to it a certain appeal. Just the announcement: I'm out of here. I'm done.

Like that bullfighter in the Hemingway story. The one who's so disgusted with his last crowd that upon departing, he makes the driver stop at the city-limits and gets out, ceremoniously removes his shoes, then claps them together, there by the side of the road. He doesn't even want to take the town's dust with him.

What pleasure that would afford. To issue the communique. 'I'm out of here. And I'm blaming you and you. And you. If you think I forgot about what you said to me back on Elizabeth Street when Ted Greenwald was sitting right there at the table, you've got another thing coming.'

Of course, there's yet another alternative: retirement. That would stop a few people in their tracks.

But you retire from a job, and this isn't a job. No gold watch. No farewell dinner. And there are never any festschrifts… not for the likes of us moral spendthrifts. Or immoral.

Every once in a while you do hear of, say, a painter announcing their retirement. That usually means they can't afford paint anymore. Or canvas, or stretchers. Stretchers will kill you. In fact, what they're really sick of may not be reusing those stretchers over and over. What they can no longer abide is the sight of all those folded-up paintings, the ones they've been demounting for decades now. Piled up in the corners, leaning stacks of them, teetering towers, taking over more and more of the loft. But even if they stop, what are they going to do with all of those pictures? Unstretched, unseen, untouched for years and years? Another Collyer brother, or sister, each and every one of those artists.

So, maybe non compos mentis is the way to go. As if we will have a choice. To be entirely clueless when it comes to how far we've fallen, what could be better? There'll we be, happily beavering away at our little desk, tucked away in our room at the home, knocking out dreadful little ditties. Perhaps the same one every day, over and over.

The pleasure we get from putting the words down on the page and moving them around, there's nothing like it. And we'll feel that feeling, we'll savor it to our hearts' delight, because no one will care if we're repeating ourselves. We won't be any the wiser. That will be the last thing on our minds, because we will have lost our minds.

However, is not this just as probable: we'll be sentenced to even more of that same night terror that has been affrighting us all these years… that in fact, we are indeed repeating ourselves. That so-familiar fear which is only assuaged, or not, when in the morning light, we look back at our drafts from the evening before and – to the extent we can trust our own eyes – we try to reassure ourselves that it may not be any good, in all likelihood it isn't, but it at least it is different. Different enough. Or is it? We will never dodge that dread.

Dying in harness, instead. That's the ticket. Keep on to the end. And when it comes, I'll raise my head up from the cobble, and there on his box will be the coachman whipping my flank heedlessly, and I'll understand, indeed the day has come. I seem to be breathing my last. Someone should call for the knackering van. Yes, this is where I should be. And this is where I should end, still doubting: didn't I write this once already?

6. SPRY AND WRY

While consumed by this line of questioning – why am I even bothering with this anymore? – I was also engaged in that equally dispiriting project, previously mentioned: what to do about those bookshelves and those book piles? Further, despite having no idea whatsoever when it came to what I was doing, I'd actually begun writing and was now three or four or drafts into the process described above, though those long lists of words, almost five years' worth represented an equally daunting prospect. While I was giving it the old college try, as I worked on each list, separately and slowly in my customary fashion, proceeding through the drafts, I found myself growing more and more alarmed: what the hell was I doing here? I had no idea. This was turning into something way too familiar. That was intolerable. Repeating – worse than doing nothing at all.

Taking a break one afternoon, I happened came across a recently arrived book, the Granary edition of *I Remember*, which I'd carelessly tossed onto the nearest pile of books, of which, of course, there were just as many as ever, as tall and teetering, looming.

It wasn't that I was unfamiliar with Brainard's book. I felt I knew it well. Although, when I went back to *An Anthology of New York Poets,* I realized it wasn't in there at all. Well, his illustrations were. They so set the tone for that entire book.

When I opened *I Remember,* first I read Ron Padgett's lovely afterword. It immediately put me in mind of his equally moving and elegant memoir of Ted Berrigan, the book that directly inspired me to start writing memoirs of my own. And then I started reading the work itself and fell in love with Joe all over again. And as I did, I kept turning back to Ron's afterword and his recounting of the wondrous impact this work had upon him and all their friends when they first read it.

The shocking simplicity of what Joe Brainard had conjured: the plain-speak, American, frank, repetition. And then, behind it, with each entry's detail –apparently artless and unassuming – as they add up, the wealth of delicate feeling, and what seems now quite period detail, along with the careful laying on of irony here and here, the astonishing breadth of experience, a veritable typology of his – and our – life, lives. And all painted with those sweetly casual tonalities (correlative to the imagery and handling he shared with us in his visual art, with its forthright embrace of commercial imagery, Americana, cartoon figuration).

And then it came to me. Why not?

I could never do what he did. That heartbreaking, ineffably fluid and fluent effusion of feeling. But his organizing principle? That so very deceptively simple trope. Why not?

By now, those lists of mine now had already sprouted, as it were. They had each grown many pages longer. All of the single words had become lines. Some of the lines had expanded into stanzas.

What did I have in mind now? It was simple.

I took the latest draft of the first year's list and marked up every line. That is, I coded them. And then I made a new draft of that year's list. This new draft had every line rearranged, according to the coding I'd just applied. First, came all of the lines and stanzas that started with the word 'the.' Then came all of the lines and stanzas that started with 'and,' and then all of the ones that started with the word 'I' and then 'you' and so on.

I looked upon the damage I'd wreaked and decided I liked it.

So, I went to all of the other lists, each of the other five years', and rearranged them similarly. Once I had completed all of this rearranging, I sat down with these new groupings and worked my way through another few drafts.

But then I had another thought, and I took each year's sections that started with 'The,' pulled them out of their respective year's document and put them together in their own Word file. All five years' worth of 'The's' by themselves. And, after they divided and multiplied a bit, after a few more drafts, they became a set of poems unto themselves, all beginning with 'The.'

And then I did the same with the 'Ands' and the 'I's and the rest. And, if not chance-driven, there was in this approach an operational-imperative that called to mind my first book, that I took a liking to.

And, several dozen drafts later, here we are.

So thank you, Joe! Who I can't say I ever knew. While I must have seen him around St. Mark's, and I did visit him once in his loft, which I've written about elsewhere, we certainly weren't pals. He was from another generation.

That some of that unadorned, unaffected charm which was your signature – the way you disclosed and disarmed – that first captivated your friends and then generation after generation of devoted readers, could rub off on me, that is too much to hope for. Nevertheless, none of this could have happened without you.

You, who could have been, who should have been, indeed would have been – if we lived in a better world, a decent world – an old man by now, spry and wry, but still among us.

Some of these poems originally appeared in:

The Brooklyn Rail
Antiphony
The Arts Fuse

Thank you, Erica Hunt, Ann Pedone and John Mulrooney

Also, thanks to these poets and friends who were kind enough to share with me their thoughts regarding the topics focused on in this book's essay: Charles Alexander, Steve Clay, Kyle Dacuyan, Joe Elliott, Rob Fitterman, Ryan Fox, the late Cole Heinowitz, Mitch Highfill, Brenda Iijima, Vincent Katz, M.C. Kinniburgh, Evelyn Reilly, James Sherry and Geoff Young

About Michael Gottlieb

Michael Gottlieb is the author of twenty-two books including most recently, *Selected Poems, Mostly Clearing, What We Do: Essays for Poets, Dear All,* as well as *Memoir and Essay*, the authoritative recounting of the early days of the Language school. He was one of the editors of *Roof*, the foundational 1970s and 80s poetry magazine. He was also the publisher of Case/Casement Books (1981-1999) and started the Last Tuesday multi-media performance series at La MaMa in NYC in the 1980s. A number of his poems have been adapted for the stage, including *And We Will Never Speak of This Again, Mostly Clearing*, and *The Dust,* his poem about 9/11 which was produced on the 10th anniversary of the attacks.

To learn more: michaelgottlieb-writing.com

About chax

Founded in 1984 in Tucson, Arizona, Chax has published more than 250 books in a variety of formats, including hand printed letterpress books and chapbooks, hybrid chapbooks, book arts editions, and trade paperback editions such as the book you are holding.

Chax Press stands against all attacks on democracy, civil rights, and the dignity and self-determination of all peoples, in the USA and internationally. We stand against authoritarian government, including that which exists within supposedly democratic systems. We stand against racism and misogyny, and against all genocides, including the one being enacted presently in Gaza against the Palestinian people. We stand for equal human rights for all, and we encourage and believe in peace and love as critical to solving problems in our world.

Your support of our projects as a reader, and as a benefactor, is much appreciated. Our current mailing address is 6181 East 4th Street, Tucson, Arizona 85711-1613. You can email us at *chaxpress@chax.org.* Find CHAX online at *https://chax.org.*

Text Font: Adobe Garamond Pro
Some Display & Page Numbers: Iowan Old Style

Book Design: Charles Alexander

Book Production: KC Book Manufacturing